Selected Titles by Lynn Strongin

The Dwarf Cycle (1972)

Paschal Poem: Now in the Green Year's Turning (1976)

Toccata of the Disturbed Child (1977)

Countrywoman/Surgeon (1979)

The Sorrow Psalms: A Book of Twentieth-Century Elegy (ed.) (2006)

Albino Peacock (2008)

Spectral Freedom, Selected Poetry, Criticism, and Prose (2009)

Twin Tan Dogs, Obedience & Discipline (2010)

Dark Salt: A Brush with Genius (2011)

Orphan Thorns (2012)

Bread of the Angels (2012)

The Burn Poems (2015)

A Bracelet
of Honeybees

A Bracelet
of Honeybees

Lynn Strongin

HEADMISTRESS PRESS

ISBN-13: 978-0997914900
ISBN-10: 0997914904

Cover art © 2003 MADY ART (Marie Bourdages). *Bone Whale,* 24 x 30 inches. Collection Lyne Corriveau.

Cover & book design by Mary Meriam

PUBLISHER
Headmistress Press
60 Shipview Lane
Sequim, WA 98382
Telephone: 917-428-8312
Email: headmistresspress@gmail.com
Website: headmistresspress.blogspot.com

Deborah: This one's for you

Contents

-3- Gospel Gossip

-4- The Honeybee Suite

Introduction

When Lynn Strongin's manuscript, *The Burn Poems,* arrived unsolicited at Headmistress Press' back door, I was on retreat in a barren landscape trying to finish my own manuscript. Yet, once I picked it up, I truly couldn't put it down. I was captivated with her story—now, an older lesbian poet, surviving with the disabling remnants of a childhood bout with polio, educated in New York City, with memorable years spent in the southern US and in Berkeley, now living in Canada. But even more than her wide-arcing narrative, I was mesmerized by her lush, always surprising imagery; the wonderful playfulness of her language; and her erudite insertions of location and literature. We published *The Burn Poems* in 2015. And then Lynn sent us another manuscript to consider.

And so, we are thrilled to present, *A Bracelet of Honeybees,* Strongin's second book with Headmistress Press. Like the first, *Honeybees* struts Strongin's signature genius with language while picking up on the narrative of *The Burn Poems* with braided themes of aging, pain, and sexuality. She harkens back to her own childhood with offerings of secrets and confessions to her doppelganger doll: "It was a bad day/ doll was carrying too much reality."

Headmistress editor Rita Mae Reese describes the book this way: "It's like Emily Dickinson meets Elizabeth Bishop, with a dash of Matthea Harvey for good measure." No emotion, notion, or possibility is missing in these sharp-witted, sometimes twisted, poems. Strongin writes despairing lines such as "all nights are hospital nights" and "In my childhood all cities were London bombed by the Germans" alongside praiseful stanzas such as "Unseen fire/ Reflected in your round face/ my ample, deep desire."

Here I give to you, reader, this treasure. It is full of honey and sting.

Risa Denenberg
Headmistress Press
August, 2016

Comments Mama made could be voiced gently
but they had their sting.
I wore them about my wrist all day,
like a bracelet of honeybees.

-1-

PENCIL-BOX DARKNESS

Twelve, upon the Hill

I have rapid pulse   thru the ceiling.
Uneven heartbeat, elder man pumping iron, a transport beyond.
I hold within my breast a bird, imprisoned quail, wire veins, tensile.

Twelve-year-old upon the hill   of hell.
From my height I hear girlhood's tolling bell,
A Holbein child nailed.

Something isolating, treacherous as first orgasm,
Cuts to the quick.
Doll, Doll, we are in the thick of it.

Intimate

Doll, so much of you will be lost in translation.
I'd put you back on my candlewick bedspread, spread in my sepia bedroom.
I am nine. Same age as you, doll, in Oyster-colored satin petticoats
        arrayed, protruding beneath your candle-colors dress, wax,
        tulip brown.
You & I are out on a wild limb   what grabs at the heart
is a light bulb in a bare room, same gray of dead grass & sticks
        coming out   of snow.
People coming & going leaving footprints they cannot gather when
        they return.

The hospital. No longer has my doll-
        rouge cheeks. Now calls owl: backdrop sky,
        stage cloth, parchment scroll. Hospital gown, on, off.
Act like Gloomy the Camel till we get together, parents & I.
Suwanee preening feathers, catching reflections.
We're born to economize on postage, old coin.

What stabs at us
        tightens around our spirit like a wasp waist: skinnier. Crueler
        is the over-lit room, 100-watt light bulb glaring out of ceiling.
People do return for forgotten footprints, shadows fail to find them.
Every little flaw, brown patch, an affront flames up, then down, brown.
Gloom always weaves its way back into tapestry.

Not quite day when we head off. Doll, you won't let go of me.
The real treasure we cannot trade in: old figurines bring scant cash.
Canopy tours are wealth in a tulip poplar, Pennsylvania, 35
        feet off ground facing one's first ever zip line.

Cuts to the Quick

When I come to the iron red door of morning
Still missing legs, you unfindable,
By fires that have been set upon ice,
I make it with codeine
Which helps me regain voice.

At dawn, I throw open the day, opening shop.
Low on firelighters: Even sunrise is cold.
Bent over double-entry keeping the books.
You come to me like oil on olives,
Do few things with childlike glee.

Chestnuts put at the foot of your cot
To ward off spider bites to toes.
We're beginning to lose our sweetness.
When the duvet zipper breaks & it's tough to extricate the duvet.
It boggles your mind.

Violet lids
Ashen
You can wave an organdy wand, but still . . .
Turning like an encyclical
Bicycle of morning . . . still it quick-cuts close to clear-cutting.
What seamstress can sew a green glass eye into a socket?
What surgeon can slip an eyeball back
For flawless vision?
The generous heart that forgives does not stockpile.

Graphite piles profile nightfall
& you go with plow, Doll, over that luminous silver hill:
Nancy, Abigail, Nell into the wild night of old age.

While in dollhouse & my room, ancient tobacco-colored bureaus
Lose a handle.
Sepia light turns wood dowels asymmetrical, makes a killing in chiaroscuro.

Bleached Porcelain

White wheat bleeds skyward in my dream:
The ward-flower stiffens in ice despite
Steam heat knocking.

Doll, I come, I run, slipping on warship clothing
In battle lights.
Afternoon:
Freak-out
Island living.
Lights out like a hedgehog underground without warning.

Warning lights
Always
On. Braces & crutches hung on a nail from a polio childhood.

Mourning clothes are easier: black shawl, high-buttoned
Laced boots,
A scarf that looks as if you've pulled it on, on the way out the door to
Catch a lorry.

Once you belonged to the circus, you ran away,
Turning volumes as a child does clay-based shiny fairytales. Inwardly
she is raging,
Outwardly tapered fingers move, paging.

The Zany Doll

       nuttier than a fruitcake, that said "Mama."
The porcelain doll in grandmother's boudoir.
One morning I found her head could turn, her hands were crazed like a German-
Bombed city. In my childhood all cities were London bombed by the Germans.
The doll-sown Dixie South was clay.
The one who wasn't a clothespin-
Nanny. The Federal Doll was argent.
But no one kept watch over anyone.

When the house burned,
The black bleak skeletons of dolls began
Dancing
Writhing in flame
Like children on hospital cots in pain.
Like Catholic kids down South in church pews squirming.

There was a snaky feel to the whole thing
Like rap dancing
Like wringing the neck of a chicken
Like black blood spilt
When someone killed someone.
The soldier that did not burn was tin.
The one that melted to the core was lead.
The sky was a pewter lid clamped on.

Secrets Withheld

All nights are hospital nights:
Vertical & horizontal crying
Lasting Impressions, waterfall card workshops
Swings of the pendulum
How am I to tell folk that one moment I am ready to close shop,
Then take God to tea
For a clay day

Late delivery:
Some ships come back   some never return from sea
Sky the color of streaky bacon
There, you're in the lanes of the city, the highways & hedges
But where can you find me?
Wearing stockings meant for a doll?
That thin withal? Secrets I can & cannot tell thee, Doll.

A Marionette on Strings Was Your Forebear

For the workshop bring stamps, scissors, trimmers, inks,
Embossing powders. If desire does not have a hole, it will soon
Become a jug of wisdom, buzzing like a hive.

I have told you all my secrets now, Doll, except one:
Double-jointed, a marionette on strings was your forebear
Operated by a puppet master.

Stage is set for a miracle to unfold.
Doll with long black stockings would not wear stiletto shoes.
She chooses words for primary furniture: never crossing legs,
No petit bourgeois Bayou woman.

Doll you have a megawatt smile & green almond eyes.
Ten thousand jump rope turns later, taken off the block,
I negotiate life for my child: wild, kinky-curled still on the block.
She is beyond the citywide crack epidemic, or is she?

Ours no home of excess which would be without caress.
Energy of a hive, seductive warmth yet discipline:
Spine of the scriptures' architectures.

My homes agree in gender.
All women weighting like gold leaves. A Jewish child.
I ask doll behind soap bubbles' degree of perfection.

Off-Duty

Off duty, Doll comes back to Old Westport,
Peels flower wallpaper
Concealing fragile, ancient customs slip.

Moving thru a pencil box darkness.
Butterscotch,
But stark: Burnt vanilla. Black umbrella of old schoolrooms.

Morning means moving thru various levels of fatigue,
Being only one doll,
One feather boat to put up on the shelf, one cap to uncloak.

Like a flower
Coming into
Semi-darkness, interrupted light. She speaks to herself.

I discover books I meant to hawk: Small valises, book-boxes from India
Strapped with silver & my doll –
Beyond repair. She cannot speak or lock hands.

Where apples were brighter than firelighters, boys in trees who walk,
& there was talk of chalking up victories till we were out of chalk.

In Trees, on Seas, Rove Men

Everyone is confused, abashed,
Boys are walking in trees,
Floating on seas.

Where is hope for you & me, Doll in damask
Like a gas mask.
One can only ask,
Where mercy?

I Didn't Attend Your Silent Auction

I was on the auction block déjà.
I saw Fire Bars in trees
Dalmatians barking wondrously
Ships sailing elm-skies.

My heart was up there for hire.
Burning like Alderwoods behind counters.
Unseen fire
Reflected in your round face, my ample, deep desire.

I go the path straight & narrow
My love straight, keen as an arrow.

Sacrilegious Diagnosis

Did Matron, cross herself
When she said
At the cot of some child (I was one):

"Two useless limbs"? Doll, none of yours working perfectly
Are worth a penny dropping, the price of admission.
Handsome, in stark clothing, you gleam like a new dime.

A child with two stick limbs. Even her. Even him.
Milk-colored meat her face, that jaw line of a shovel.
All roads lead to hell, none to home.

My cruel attendants are oxygen tanks, "Eagle Propane" at the beside.
Roll up the lino of the ward: Lord, Super Novae are exploding.
Hospital ward, fall blue evening.

Gypsy Rose has a cairn in her dark hair
& signed my sister's diploma.
I'm rolling dice between my invisible hands.

I'm praying for a river
In this dry dark
This umber nether

World
This breathless
Ether

Where stars ignite, birds breaking dark
Mountain silence & wolves bark.

-2-

BEDSITTERS AND OTHER SORROWS

In the Carriage House

Rose Manor, behind the rectory, I'll live as an old woman,
Thinks doll, clothespin thin.
Behind the chapel girls are walking trees.
From far away
As Florence Lake
The dwarf optician drives in each day, cataracts milk over
& fog-gray his eyes.
He is not blind
Except for dawn & dusk driving.
He builds his own eternity:
The lenses,
Tiffany lamps he made himself until recently, the eyeball tree.
Behind the retina is hell.
But before
A web, which casts a spell.
I live in The Glenshiel,
Back of the rectory
Where men walk in trees slowly.
My own infinity builds with night, dims by day.
Always doll, caught in the oval mirror you are watching me.
Mirror, au revoir until I'm called away.
In the carriage house given me,
That once stabled horses in mews:
Equine, palm & ebony, a stone's shift from sea.

In My Retirement
(she speaks to the walls around her)

Rather than follow swooping flocks of birds
I will study migrations of language
From north to south,

Lacing
The mouth
Of the sweet lost.

I, Amsterdam
Uncover your eyes
The tail is pinned to the donkey.

Clamber, sweet mind monkey.
God carved all outside, Lamb, Oryx, Oriole
& all (including Angels washing feet) & mule inside me.

Poblano Peppers

Doll bought little blues—the florist could not name them—so many
        they cost the earth!
Whole bunch
Not just one stalk
Flowers today that set me back thirty
No name for this time
People do not divide over differing economic philosophy
No time to dream of a bedsitter
Although we do.

Meantime at the bus shelter, no room for two or three.
We: just out in the cold rain. Who are we?
The women of the neighborhood.
We are Sandy, Patti, & Jean at the bus shelter on a Friday morning.
We are the women whose husbands left, whose birth was in Korea,
Whose education the States & home Canada.

The windows are blown out of the bus shelter.
Two thin sheets of plastic & won't be mended till Halloween.
In disrepair, they make the women clutching small bundles tied with string
More forsaken. Doll included, she sketches a poem:

We are the disabled, the one woman who is eldest invited to live
with her daughter, which she will do since travel is now off
the chart to the other island. But she will bring a sheepdog
to bind   parting shot, loving swing: Her parting wounds.

It Has Been a Long, Endless Day

for Doll.
The women at their quilting whispering
Like water running.
I pray
No more pain for Shelby.
The mystical exercise in pain, not the futility
Of pursuing another catalogue in process
With bar code & numerals
Aligned like gray
Soldiers in a ghost army.
But there is no answer
& sometimes God comes
Lightning in a bottle
So quickly.

Bad Day

It was a bad day
Doll was carrying too much reality
So dropped it. The valise contents darkened the wood at her feet.

Eagle Propane parked outside in first winter rain.
The bus driver was depressed although still wearing shorts.
But not for much longer. People in the village felt the first gray,
Bent heads, knifed each other with elbows, children & birds did cry.
Briars in hair.

Briar Mansion & Sunset House closed early, it turned out prematurely.
Folk looked to shoes
Pervasively as pores of stone
Drinking rain.
The bus shelter, visible from top of hill
Filled with twilight rather than day
An opened book gave no fresh news: tired, stale as day old bread.
Little light was shed upon text.

What next?
Janey had died recently, dinner burned, the kettle bottom black as char.
Now Shelby
Hugs shawls about her
Abdomen engraved in pain again
Another morning is likely coming,
There is a pall.
God arrives slowly, or not at all.

The Back Alleys of Victorian London's East End

Doll flicks the tulip lightbulb on frosted milk.
Amid smoke, mud, & shadows where laundry trembles in air,
Egon, her beloved friend, affirms her mother's infirmity.
Traveling, traveling
Embracing dilemmas of culture, history
All things
In a world almost vanished
Like the form in the mirror
Doll clasps her bosom woman friend
To her slim chest
As one does
A civil war
Bandage
To a wound
An ancient wound, a winter one.

The Darling Foundry

Stands in its circle of stone. Doll sits on her pillow of bone linen.
The great thing about those antique myths is there's a very human side.
Run the train against the wall.
Tell all.
The work of a genius on a very high level:
Are you up to this huge creative challenge?
Shelby, when rains have come, we each wear green veils, each private.
Anne saw pygmies either in a dream or at the World's Fair.
Her parents wore blue & orange, fair colors?
Her memory is pathologically beautiful, a mirror, her nurse a
Scotswoman.
They had uniformed nannies
In those dark mineshaft days,
& She & my first–cousin, one year apart, Anne's only friend
Rocked in rocking ducks.
O Ducks. Darling Foundry. Birds & animals of my youth.
Even good harmless things can turn out to be rigged to do harm in
This life, to cut like a knife.
But clay of angels runs in our veins. Pygmies might have been a
nursery school outing: no preaching soul the golden rule.
How cruel that there was a lamp on top of a 3-foot fridge:
        this was her Paradise, her Yule.

The Impermanence of the Physical World

Dismays her. What was once a glass cup holds rose ashes in decay.
Glass is comforting: its clarity. Like your eyes, doll, green, glassy.

What remains of yesterday's weather?
They hold each other
Ice & fire
The endless night
The letter with a Yorkshire postmark
All comes home with nightfall balled into a dark wad of clay.

She is almost seventy years of age. That's a long time for a Miss Hickory to live.
No one has it easy with darkness coming on.
Dressed in two sweaters, one blue jacket, her mother darts out the door for Norway.
She takes refuge in story
As though it were a cave.
Oysters for dinner were fine.

Her companion, Flinty, sleeps like a lexicon upon a pillow.
Bunched up dreaming of silver spurs, fish & chips, soon you will be begging for a jar
Though I am no steward.
I am your love.
The moon floats off like a marshmallow, but we are uncushioned
By thoughts of tomorrow.

Went Square Dancing

What a dirndl
Pin swirl
Shaking down the acorn
A hair-raising event
Blackberry cloud
Rising from gold soil
Went square dancing my elbow-in elbow
With this soul
Old fezzi-curls
A natural take on the dark carnival
A song for no dancing chicken
But a rooster
Edgy, your mother's wristwatch was a crystal clouded with use
From the darkened temple of longing
Heart's open spaces
Where a mother disappeared as bipolar: opal ruse
& a brilliant ear emerged
O fire landscape
Eloquent addiction
But a bracelet of honeybees is not glass:
It's gloss.

Down the Road

If she had her druthers
Doll'd be going out to dinner rather than on these *mothers* laced with codeine.
Yesterday, the courier went & came.
"Redelivery" (the owl narrates) is a life story.
Still there is Moxie.

Duff motors South on down the road splashing leaf shadows like champagne.
Rumble seat sprung
Hat on with rose feather boa
Out of her babyhood black
Large lady
Dread is no carriage: fear is a marriage of history & future.

I mean to say, one can't just get in & head down the road waving at boys.
Glad creatures & grinning from one side of the map to the other.
Check precise location: Catching shadows of trees,
The sun in Cleo's eyes while her memory of being a baker
Reels on from spool-to-spool & my books come wrapped in environmentally
        safe peanuts which dissolve in water.

Rather be out to wine & dine rather than on these mothers' pills
Chockablock full of codeine.
The summer people are gone,
The shadows fill gutters, air wells
The color of duffle bag,
Sky drinks from a rainspout,
While that old hag Pain slings her bag over her shoulders,
Shuffles on down & Cleo drives like a bat out of hell under
A cranberry moon.

Five-Fingered Fern

Priests & Magi as trees walking.
Children as puppets talking.
Most magical you are,
Five-fingered fern.

She brought out the old mulberry-scented Sobranies.
God forbid they take up smoking again:
>   two aging women's women in a country outside the pale:
>   silver-tarnished, family silver burned grey, luminous.
How Flinty supported her career:
Bought her paper at every turn
Clips
Fasteners
The slow burn back into the space beyond the hall with the maple doll.
The Sobranies (the soprano voice inside me) I kept all these years.

All
Held in locked lips until I spill
To porcelain
To rouged circles
To passion subdued thru it within & beyond the acorn-squall.
In the cupboard
Out of the closet   at last, not least:
Blood-roses on wall.
I kiss the five-fingered fern: whisper
Secrets you tell your doll.

Gospel Gossip

she calls it, because they live by it.
It stands in relief like cameos
To the issues of home.
Whether to enter a "Home," The Glenshiel or some other
       euphemistically named.
Like Eucharist she takes the wafer daily of the old & lone.
How quickly a series of evenings so hardly turned.
Who has what right over whom?

Sawing in dark
Like a small deer
Or little hunting fox
On leash

I mourn the unforeseen turn: diminished coffers, deficits multiplying
       like tumors in all provinces.
Only this morning, chatting at a bus shelter too small for three &
       one wheelchair-bound—the talk mainly about when the
       pension comes how she'll replace the worn area carpet

Into a wall
Like the Wailing Wall
One crosses to by Yom Kippur Bridge
Into a strong
Unspeakable,
Unspeakable stone: seductive, forbidding
Like secrets you whisper to your doll. Her alone.

I Go Into a Dark Country

Doll, in your pinstriped apron
For nocturnal baking. She who must be obeyed brings home African squash
Hard as a nut.
I can see their cream running.
"I'm debating eating my second pluot" she stands in the door, winding
                    herself, not like spaghetti as she did when young,
But sinuous.
I think—but do not say, *make up your mind.*
In my early forties I was one of a series of ten drawings.
Now the darkness is covering my limbs.
Water lapping
The way eyelet must have covered me as a baby.
Are old women very old babies? Not on your life! Fie!
I sat at the bus stop listening to the old women with wonderment
Weaving gossip
Gospel gossip
Like knitting covers, stringing rosaries
As if rosaries could be woven
Or the cover finally done
The last needle removed
The soul & body numb.

-3-

GOSPEL GOSSIP

Nightly the Fire Alarm Sounds

        which lasts till morning.
The parchment book is open to page
One
Haircut for my doll
One eye blue, one green
One clouded, one vision-
Airy
One toward history
Hers
The kind with metal cups & saucers
Matchstick sized windows
Stop at the blue
Go at the green.
She's a goer
But has run into a problem:
No one, nothing in her world can stop the billowing flames
Like the cancer at the end for Carolyn, Jennifer, Anne.

She beats it back.
She tears up rugs—the China Dalmatian does not take up barking
        nor break from his dollhouse leash: She is extreme, opulent
        as a lush. The floor burns, the baby's initialed dish. None of
        this is her wish.
She pushes fire away with her hands. It smocks her as though she
        were an artist painting it. But all around her remain dumb &
        numb.
Skulls cry for salvation. She stops her ears as the flames eat them.

Codeine Is Cold Comfort

Her bed-fellow, bed-woman.
Don't comfort me with apples
In Mama Morphia's arms
(thinks doll).
Like smoke curled round a chimney,
Like the way Ivy twines,
Narcotic-Nona wraps arms about me
Then dreams.
Late dolly,
From whom she stalked away,
Still talking to her under breath.
Now the lid's on night. Ducks bark.
As a child I was unafraid of the dark.
But now seventy on at my lips—I resist drink
Thirsting
Yet sufficiently
Sated with Hallelujahs to call it a day.

Does Doll Speak in Alto or Soprano?

The last decade of my life has had no snow.
You gave me access to excess material at the Bodleian Library.

Spilling over,
I gave it caress.
I remembered the doll dress,
The fear of going crazy I had as a child.
Did other children have this? Like fear of mice in small places,
        of firecrackers?
I ate Pond's cold cream with a milked
Air
A smile close to the Cheshire cat's smirk
Which disappeared with the dark.

Does a doll dream in English or in Russian?
Russian I would imagine since I am of Slavic origin,
Jewish, yet Christ-haunted like the South,
Like a funeral parlor haunted by flowers,
Like night when I am spooked out
With fear of losing
Your hand in my hand
                your choir child's lips on my mouth.

Light Is Perfect Which Bringeth

Unfettered, opaque
Light is expectant
Quaint
If figures walk in trees, they are antique, ancient pain.
Doll, you know the whole thing from beginning to end.
When you begin feeling like a lighthouse keeper
& taking a Q tip to clean the knobs of your radiator, your radio,
  the spaces between your typer's keys
   it's time to get out in the freeze
   where angels are floating.

It ain't easy:
Ultrasounds & cat scans
Let's hope the ruffled waters turn calm.
North is colding up
Chilling down.
My love she merely scolds me: Yet
In between the stars
An ashen path:
Doll, doll I love you both:
A light more excellent than that, which shineth.

Doll, Is the Storm Over?

With fork-lightning, it turned us into marbly lovers.
It rocked us from cover-to-cover.
My head was a wounded bear.
I speak to you in waning health, taffeta light
Up-sky, flickering candles.
The shadow side of wealth.
Savior –

No sugaring, doll
Back to star-gazing
Blood lighthouse
Salt fire
Stars thick as in a foggy sky
Learning the ropes of Requiem
Who could brave it out, black cherry trees come to life, shining
Relapse to salvation.

At first I had seemed in free-fall:
Fear index high, Icarus tumbling thru space further, further
Reeling
Like mist traveling hurricane speed
The wall's turning cold with winter
The outlawry of boyhood
Shades me
As I run
Outlaw from my life.

Snow in the East, Fear in the West

Fast on: reading American Photo Booth.
The history of the automated photo machine.
The emotions involved in its manufacture.

Fast on, Doll: Porcelain girl, no feast.
Earliest, nerviest dawn I woke. I felt my chest. It was wet.
Where I wore a vest,
Was blood rust. In the pinhole dollhouse light. . . a bullet?

Thin as membrane the sooty rouge weskit,
The hole looked ripped burned. The sun was red as bloodsport.
Keep goodbyes short.
Doll, your hair is parted, skull vulnerable.
Daylight is hard as pure clear drinking water, cup it in your porcelain hands.

Last
Loss of day was my medic alert panic button, breaking from string.
See-Saw Marjorie Daw, one's up, one down. I saw
Fear pop like Jack-in-the Boxes
Raw.

Look what Mr Blanchflower found.
Burn up wheat. Burning thru cash hoard.
Desperate like when Gary was in a wet bed,
His leukemia so bad
His fever soared.

Now late roses circle the heart.
While Sweet Pea comes home with the best branch of Brussels sprouts.
She lays them near me against the fridge. Though rich,
Its otherworldliness touches like the touch of a hand from the opposite shore,
The other side, the glass.
With me on codeine.

It Would Be Like Setting a Trench on Fire

To leave you, doll.
There are Codas
And Soda's:
Children of Deaf adults
Siblings of Deaf adults.
Amazed,
Can I be dazzling?
Everything startles me: my own shadow
The downturn in the economy
The economical way my love turns back & frowns, or smiles,
Dimples clear as shadows in velvet
In the door.
What now can keep us going?
Not whiskey & soda
Or amber scotch,
Like one time.
Now talk in the bus shelter
Cloaks our shoulders
Gives us a cape though we are mild, even bordering on British in manner.
Brutish night closes in. Time
To hunker down.
Like kids pleading for rice on the rim of starvation.

Doll, Go to No Memory Clinic

With dark torn apart milled edges
You on the edge of night
Your memory exhausting
Autobiographical
Cruelly bright
You accumulate a diary inside a thimble.

Reflective,
Your pages are full
As a lake,
As a millwheel's
Highly reliable turns.

An abnormality of memory? Or is her brain wired in another sort of way?
She blossoms in facts, her hands touch a teacup
& it blends with milk colored
Lightbulb lit morning.

You, captive forever doll, with those pale shoes.
Like a griever at a funeral so small she is almost invisible.
No edges get worn off.
She is in mourning.

A Flashbulb Memory at Hallelujah Fork

Doll stays awake, the radio is staticky:
October 12.
Where is the lining to her blue-black coat in which she'd go to town
If she had not given up so much in life,
Become prisoner of this room.
Enthralled by detail
She will not die like humans
Or stop breathing.
She will stop recording.
Retaining on the upper story of the dollhouse
What the children together did that afternoon they were sewing
Piling teacups in the miniature sink.
She resembles E. D. on the postage stamp.
The lady of the home,
The daughter of the mother
Left a letter, carelessly. On the dollhouse table.
It knocked it over & every other thing
As though a fierce wind
Blew thru the jewel case of that home, that box, so she had to compose herself, doll
Knowing she was locked up to be captive forever in those boxes for breathing.

What Causes the Snail to Close His Valve?

What motivates Doll to close
Before sundown the house? Oblivion is a salve.
She does not respond as she did once
To that tree
Out the parlor window. The poplar.
Twilight is not as popular with her,
Yet more peculiar.

A word is a piece of furniture you move around: can sit in, stiff & painful straight spine.
Indeed, it was only yesterday.
Night.
This gives rise to floating anxieties
Like droning
Bees
Hypnotic
Enchanting.

But cloth of nightfall she lifts, rubs back & forth between two things
Gold as corncobs bit clean.
No new voiture to get in & go down the road.
The choirs in her head are sing-songing: she claps hands to her ears.
It's an old thing: she knows & does not know it.
She reads it like Braille dot-by-dot connecting history to harm
Of longing.

Has She Had a Lesion?

Is she in relapse?
Or elated when she claps her hands like birds
& lets dreams scatter like white doves
In a startlingly beautiful painting.
The task of neuroscience is to differentiate between cells & lace.
What about this crimson moving sunset? She knows not yet.
One thing undercuts the other. She has romance, loves snow & rain.
But she will recollect, collect pen & ink & put it down,
Bright as cranberry; she'll get it right.

A Prussian neurologist maps human brains.
She sets down the milk glass cup.
She wants to be left alone.
To mull over things
As one mulls old raspberry wine.

I wouldn't think of lifting the shawl over the dollhouse as one covers
A birdcage at night
& disturb the organ
In the loft
Its gold pipes
Like birches slanting toward heaven
Or the haven
The organ
Of that crystal walnut
Her brain.

The Immense Complexity of Memory

Of the stars
Thru the dollhouse moon roof,
The globe glows.
She shields her eyes with her arm as she goes.
Her skin & eyelashes are slim.
She brushes aside branches
Which shadow the west room.
The pianist of "Ideas of the North," records the Goldberg Variations.
She is trembling.
For this they could divorce us, she thinks.
She & dollboy
Who no longer acts up,
Devours two books a week,
Reflections like a crystal pond.
Recollections cut the surface
The way another wrinkle occurs in immigration.
Her brother studies the biology of mind. But locked up,
She holds her abdomen; she looks out at cobalt rain, Indigo.
She presses toward her unborn shadow-children:
Lace floating to the surface of tea.
A hallucinogen was in the tea this afternoon.

Doll, She Leaves No Footprints

In dust or home.
A residue of experience rises like the ghost of a little person's, swirls
In cones. She smiles, she can almost cup them in her hands.
You can see them in the air
Like atoms
Dancing
An anagram.
She lifts day like a church bench,
That heavy.
A cube of leather is for burial.
A cube of ice is for liquor.
Doll dusts off handprints
From books.
Some are grimed in
Like those of the cyclical poems of the seasons
In the Farmer's almanac
Presented at the time of retrieval
When she gave the white dog
His bone
The color of leukemia
Which he licked clean
& then there was no tongue
& then no dog at all
None.

Frost, the Secret Tensions of a Conflicted Family

Encrypt ice on the milk, the cream.
Beads scrim & canisters
Set on the doorstep of home at dawn. The dollhouse
Collects sun like a dipper, scooping it.
A dollhouse mouse
On wheels –
Goes a tail of grey flame.
Frost covers trees tapping on windows like gauze.
Patches of gold
On trees like kiss of God.
Trees turn.
Weather is filled with omen   women.
The sad story of the flowers
Is the florist had just been turned over to a woman from Prague
Who didn't know the ropes.
Rather than ringing a florist there, she drove the flowers up, back from the hills.
Long-traveled larkspur, button mums, sunflowers nonetheless
Arrived pristine,
Not coated with film like the dollhouse ones
Covering the tin teapot.
The frost-
Conflicted family.
Secret tensions which shone thru like bone thru skin.

Doll's Rx

Turns up late, she is short,
Out
& the room cobalt
As underwater in a boat.
Doll has laid out the tin
Plates for shining gooseberry jam
But goes back & forward as in a swing
On ropes
In some chainmail rust nail yard.
In the kitchen
Her bowl of song
Takes fire
She grabs the hallway Persian
Carpet to put it out
But stained glass
Windows it becomes.
She has taken
Her nightfall
Medication.

The Plums

Like apples, the most radiant are bruised.
She can read maps of Zagreb in them.
Wearing her damask apron embroidered with pears
Standing tall, drawing back her shoulders, she rearranges the balls of fruit.
Death has not visited these rooms in a long time.
At her Catholic cousin's
Kathryn's smile was visible in glass-topped coffin in the parlor.
The front room paneled in Cherrywood filled with cream hibiscus.
Doll's memory kept knocking
On wood
Broom broom broom.
She bore herself out of rooms
There merely blown
Rose on rose.
I'm not good at forever folding.
Toss bags.
Long division & short division: she'd learned them.
One rose was the color of sherry,
The other
The color of bantam at dawn
Crowing its crimsons thru the white dollhouse rooms.

Old Lace

Doll throws over her a mantilla filtered like sunlight into dapples
       of light and dark, old lace worn in pain and washed clean.

Her thoughts soar even when they touch base, bottom.
She has touched bottom.

She stands in doorways waving off other persons
Till they recede & disappear off the curve of the road.

One night
She lowers her hand to lift apron
Wipe tears away
But her hand is frozen
The apron is stiff as wood
As clay
Her features are still moving.

But other than that,
Where is the body?
There is the light around it,
A hoop still whirling.
There is the heartbeat
But she cannot wipe away the salt:
There is no hand.

Beyond This Night

Red deer thru this closed but unlocked door,
Doll,
I have gone nowhere
For many many years.
Stack them like half-dollar pancakes on Sunday morning.
The coat is torn, also shredding its cuffs & silk lining.
Tomorrow night I will be pining for this night back again.
My love hasn't touched me in ten years
Yet the sun rises
The earth turns
The years turn to tears
The small millwheel of dream turns.
White water falls over laps of it like feathers
Exploding
From the owl held in so long
His passion
Shot him clear
Out of the barn.
You, Doll remain mute but the locked lips are in desperation
Like the door to the cell in the house that Joan
Built.

Coffee

She sees   no coffin
To lie down in, get high apostate
Not be laid having died in   *bête noir*
Under thumbnail sketch of moon.

Live a Little

Wear washable suede.
Doll wears cords. She remembers having a spinal tap when young.
Sips white tea with Amanda-Flinty at the crest of town this twilit-noon.

One dream-space out of dollhouse.
Knife shadows of winter elbow in. Mobs jostle in banks, shoe stores.
Hot hot tea goes down.

Doll wears
Chocolate
The color of her hair.

She owns her soul
She may be strong black coffee strong enough to stand on its own.
Straight ahead, brown betty.

Looks to her left, to her right
You harvest me, firetruck
You harvest me, puppet
She thinks. In fright, her lips close. The firefighter
In glass is no rose. Vertical, horizontal child / woman.

The bombers in brass
Pass before her eyes.

She sees the last autumnal cameo
(flashes back to the "Darling" foundry) the cameo milks over
Framing lovers on the swing-set
Then blots her white tea with her napkin, rises,
In ash-colored noon-twilight,
Follows Amanda Flinty home, dragging one foot
With transparent ball on chain.

-4-

THE HONEYBEE SUITE

Amelia

       shearing through clouds towards the Thames
Behind a mirage of home
Goggles on
Sees Saturn's circles, angels' haloes, honeybees in their hive
So close to danger

Inside,
Hair windblown   classic: modern
Milkweed clouds   blown   apart
Coppery stands—London, St Paul
Blitz in its curved ship bones
Barely earth, as I land
Sparrows scattering
Without trace of blood
No beheading
Only hedges in their heyday
Falcons
For wrapping
Stone earth
White snow
No perfect three-point: one wing up   one scraping ground
Love
Freezing as xylocaine   eyes bright with tears

Written in Water

(for D)

as I'd never write your love,
But the wards, those crucifixion rows of cots,
Fighting back tears & losing, I sing.

I cannot do the things for you I want
So I dream   a celestial bookshop
Here, all quarters, especially poetry, arrive on time
Or are early births
Calling the midwife often—
        she presses forward, heavy wooden crucifix
        thumping, thumping her chest.

Some births occur at the old Ormond Street, some at the great Old London.
Those are the more complicated ones—
Emergency C-sections
Twins
Complex like our love, a web of delicate tracery upon the night sky.
A heart hums like a hive of honeybees.

But that was back in childhood.
She needs it now.
Just as, looking down, she needs girlhood hands—
        to tie a knot, to reach a jar,
To make love—

Sappho in a wimple
Softly, softly rocking
Humming.

Amelia

        I didn't mean, shearing down among clouds
To pass you
Wingtips brushed, touched
Blowing sparks as from coal   London on a dark night
The thickest pea soup in twenty-five years
Torches of midwives on bikes   flares hardly seen thru the fog
You could reach out & not touch a sister's fingers
So no wonder, in coal-burning London, below us by less than
        a quarter mile, I nearly missed you.
But I didn't. That's the true
Sorrow

Near collapse
A year and some under eighty still struggling
Ready for the ecstasy of throwing in the mop
Giving in

Orphaned Voices

Float in silence
After falling snow
Before the snow plow turns over its motor, keyed, again
A text of sky
With birds
Looking down the barrel of gun
The cross hairs capturing a lily, dreamed
A rabbi of stone
A stage of blown glass
Up & down horizontal landscape
Daring to traverse cello ground
I have dropped a note
To you
But the blizzard blows over it.

Doesn't death always march with a Christian shield of
Silence. Orphaned in the ward
I pictured the teepee mother built in the yard for her son
Five feet from the wooden steps, sagging in the middle
Of the Colorado shack.

I have come to you
At the end
Of the storm.

Lynn Strongin in 2016. Photo by Deborah Munro.

About the Author

Born in New York City into a middle-class Jewish family, Lynn Strongin contracted polio at age 12 and was confined to the New York State Rehabilitation Center for 6 months; then continued her education through the city's homeschooling program. Following high school, she attended the Manhattan School of Music; received a degree in literature from Hunter College and an M.A. at Stanford University; and studied for her doctorate at the University of New Mexico.

In the 1960s, she collaborated with Denise Levertov in politically active Berkeley. She has taught, and her work has been taught, in college classrooms throughout the United States. Strongin has published more than a dozen books and her work appears in at least 30 anthologies. She is the recipient of two PEN grants, an American Association of University Women (ASUW) Fellowship, and an NEA Creative Writing Grant. *Countrywoman/Surgeon* was a candidate for the Elliston Award in 1979 and *Spectral Freedom* was nominated for a Pulitzer Prize in 2009.

In 1979, Strongin moved to Canada for what was supposed to be a short stay. She remained and currently lives in British Columbia.

"Very much the work of a true poet."
—Denise Levertov

"One thinks of Emily Dickinson more than any other poet."
—Cassandra Robison

"Lynn Strongin is the most innovative, exciting poet writing today.
—Hugh Fox

Headmistress Press Books

Lovely - Lesléa Newman
Teeth & Teeth - Robin Reagler
How Distant the City - Freesia McKee
Shopgirls - Marissa Higgins
Riddle - Diane Fortney
When She Woke She Was an Open Field - Hilary Brown
God With Us - Amy Lauren
A Crown of Violets - Renée Vivien tr. Samantha Pious
Fireworks in the Graveyard - Joy Ladin
Social Dance - Carolyn Boll
The Force of Gratitude - Janice Gould
Spine - Sarah Caulfield
Diatribe from the Library - Farrell Greenwald Brenner
Blind Girl Grunt - Constance Merritt
Acid and Tender - Jen Rouse
Beautiful Machinery - Wendy DeGroat
Odd Mercy - Gail Thomas
The Great Scissor Hunt - Jessica K. Hylton
A Bracelet of Honeybees - Lynn Strongin
Whirlwind @ Lesbos - Risa Denenberg
The Body's Alphabet - Ann Tweedy
First name Barbie last name Doll - Maureen Bocka
Heaven to Me - Abe Louise Young
Sticky - Carter Steinmann
Tiger Laughs When You Push - Ruth Lehrer
Night Ringing - Laura Foley
Paper Cranes - Dinah Dietrich
On Loving a Saudi Girl - Carina Yun
The Burn Poems - Lynn Strongin
I Carry My Mother - Lesléa Newman
Distant Music - Joan Annsfire
The Awful Suicidal Swans - Flower Conroy
Joy Street - Laura Foley
Chiaroscuro Kisses - G.L. Morrison
The Lillian Trilogy - Mary Meriam
Lady of the Moon - Amy Lowell, Lillian Faderman, Mary Meriam
Irresistible Sonnets - ed. Mary Meriam
Lavender Review - ed. Mary Meriam

www.ingramcontent.com/pod-product-compliance
Lightning Source LLC
Chambersburg PA
CBHW060350050426
42449CB00011B/2907